Duncles 50 Great

GW01090682

Photographs from the Father Francis Brown (1880-1960) collection
have been used with the kind permission of the administrators.
Cover photo by Pat O'Dea: - Traditional Music at the Fleadh Cheoil,
Clonmel, Co. Tipperary. Courtesy of Bord Fáilte.

Layout, Design and Typesetting by Grace O'Halloran.
Cover by Niche Design, Dublin.

Printed by Watermans, Cork.

The Band Played 'Waltzing Matilda' © Roberton Brown & Associates
Grace Words & Music O'Meara/O'Meara © Asdee Music
Sonny's Dream Copyright Control
The Streets of New York by Liam Reilly © Bardis / River Music Ltd.

Ossian Publications Ltd., P.O. Box 84, Cork, Ireland

OMB 80

ISBN 0 946005 61 3

GRACE

G
As we gather in the chapel here
      C   D
In old Kilmainham jail,
C   G
I think about the last few weeks,
            Am   D
Oh will they say we failed.
         G
From our school days they have told us
        C   D
We must yearn for liberty
C   G
Yet all I want in this old place
D   G
Is to have you here with me.

CHORUS:
    D
Oh Grace just hold me in your arms
   C   G
And let this moment linger
     C   G
Then take me out at dawn
Am   D
And I will die

With all my love I'll place
           C   G
This wedding ring upon your finger
     C   G
There won't be time to share our love
    D   G
For we must say goodbye.

Now I know it's hard for you my love,
To ever understand
The love I bear for these brave men,
My love for this brave land,
But when Padraic called me to his side
Down in the G.P.O.,
I had to leave my own sick bed,
To him I had to go.
REPEAT CHORUS

Now as the dawn is breaking on this day,
Mum, as I walked out,
My thoughts will be of you, and I'll write
Some words upon the walls,
So everyone will know,
I loved you so much that I could
See his blood upon the rose.
REPEAT CHORUS

Words & Music O'Meara/O'Meara
© Asdee Music

A NATION ONCE AGAIN

G
When boyhood's fire was in my blood,
    C   D   G
I read of ancient freemen,
For Greece and Rome, who bravely stood,
         C   Am   D
Three hundred men and three men.
And then I prayed I yet might see
       C   G
Our fetters rent in twain,
       C   Am   D
And Ireland long a province, be
   G   D   G
A nation once again.

CHORUS:
     G   C
A nation once again,
     Am   D
A nation once again,
     G   Em   C   D
And Ireland long a province, be
   G   D   G
A nation once again.

And from that time through wildest woe,
That hope has shone a far light;
Nor could love's brightest summer glow
Outshine that solemn starlight.
It seemed to watch above my head,
In forum, field and fane;
Its angel voice sang round my bed,
'A nation once again.'
REPEAT CHORUS

It whispered too that freedom's ark
And service high and holy,
Would be profaned by feeling dark
And passions vain and lowly;
For freedom comes from God's right hand,
And needs a godly train;
And righteous men must make our land
'A nation once again.'
REPEAT CHORUS

So as I grew from boy to man,
I bent me to that bidding -
My spirit of each selfish plan
And cruel passion ridding;
For thus, I hoped some day to aid -
Oh, can such hope be vain?
When my dear country shall be made
A nation once again.
REPEAT CHORUS

THE BAND PLAYED 'WALTZING MATHILDA'

```
D         G         D                              A      D
When I was a young man I carried my pack, and lived the free life of a rover.
              G            D                          A       D
From the Murrays green basin to the dusty outback I waltzed my Mathilda all over.
     A       G          D      A                              G       D
Then in nineteen fifteen the country said, 'Son, it's time to stop rambling there's work to be done,
            G        D                        A        D
And they gave me a tin hat and they gave me a gun, and they sent me away to the war.
              G         D                          A
And the band played 'Waltzing Mathilda' as our ship pulled away from the quay,
     G              D       G   D      A   D
And amidst all the cheers, flag-waving and tears, we sailed off to Gallipoli.
```

How well I remember that terrible day how the blood stained the sand and the water
And how in that town that they called Suvla Bay we were butchered like lambs at the slaughter.
Johnny Turk he was ready, he primed himself well he chased us with bullets, he rained us with shells
And in five minutes flat he'd blown us all to hell nearly blew us right back to Australia.
But the band played 'Waltzing Mathilda' as we stopped to bury our slain
We buried ours and the Turks buried theirs then we started all over again.

Now, those that were left, well we tried to survive in a mad world of blood, death and fire
And for ten weary weeks I kept myself alive but around me the corpses piled higher.
Then a big Turkish shell knocked my arse over head and I woke up in my hospital bed
I saw what it had done and I wished I was dead, never knew there were worse things than dying.
For I'll go no more waltzing Mathilda all around the green bush far and near
For to hump tent and pegs, a man needs both legs no more waltzing Mathilda for me.

So they collected the cripples, the wounded, the maimed and they shipped us back home to Australia
The armless, the legless, the blind, the insane, those proud wounded heroes of Suvla.
And as our ship pulled into Circular Quay, I looked at the place my legs used to be
And thank Christ there was no one there waiting for me to grieve and to mourn and to pity.
And the band played 'Waltzing Mathilda' as they carried us down the gangway
But nobody cheered, they just stood there and stared then turned all their faces away.

And now every April I sit on my porch and I watch the parade pass before me
And I watch my old comrades, how proudly they march, renewing old dreams of past glory.
And the old men march slowly, all bent, stiff and sore the tired old men from a forgotten war
And the young people ask, 'what are they marching for?' and I ask myself the same question.
And the band played 'Waltzing Mathilda' and the old men answer to the call
But year after year their numbers get fewer some day no one will march there at all.

Last chorus, sung to the tune of 'Waltzing Mathilda':

Waltzing Mathilda, Waltzing Mathilda, who'll come a-waltzing Mathilda with me
And their ghosts may be heard as you pass the Billabong, who'll come a-waltzing Mathilda with me?

Young Australian Sailors having their hair cut, 1924

BUNCLODY

D
Oh, were I at the moss-house,
      A   D
Where the birds do increase,
    A   D
At the foot of Mount Leinster,
 G   A
Or some silent place,
           D
By the streams of Bunclody,
  G   A
Where all pleasures do meet,
 D
And all I would ask,
    A   D
Is one kiss from you sweet.

If I was in Bunclody
I would think myself at home,
'Tis there I would have a sweetheart,
But here I have none.
Drinking strong liquor
In the height of my cheer,
Here's a health to Bunclody
And the lass I love dear.

The cuckoo is a pretty bird,
It sings as it flies,
It brings us good tidings
And tells us no lies.
It sucks the young bird's eggs
To make its voice clear,
And the more it cries cuckoo,
The summer draws near.

If I was a clerk
And could write a good hand,
I would write to my true love
That she might understand,
I am a young fellow
That is wounded in love,
That lived by Bunclody
But now must remove.

If I was a lark
And had wings I could fly,
I would go to yon arbour
Where my love she does lie,
I'd proceed to yon arbour
Where my true love does lie,
And on her fond bosom
Contented I would die.

'Tis why my love slights me
As you may understand,
That she has a freehold
And I have no land,
She has great store of riches
And a large sum of gold,
And everything fitting
A house to uphold.

So adieu my dear father,
Adieu my dear mother,
Farewell to my sister,
Farewell to my brother;
I am bound for America,
My fortune to try,
When I think of Bunclody,
I'm ready to die.

THE CROPPY BOY

G   C
'Twas early, early in the spring,
D   G
The birds did whistle and sweetly sing,
           C   G
Changing their notes from tree to tree,
      D   G
And the song they sang was old Ireland free.

'Twas early, early on a Tuesday night,
When the Yeomen cavalry gave me a fright,
To my misfortune and sad downfall,
I was taken prisoner by Lord Cornwall.

'Twas in his guard-house where I was laid,
And in his parlour I was tried,
My sentence passed and my spirits low,
When to New Geneva I was forced to go.

When I was marching over Wexford Hill,
Oh, who could blame me to cry my fill
I looked behind, I looked before,
But my tender mother I ne'er saw no more.

Farewell father and mother too,
And sister Mary I have none but you
And for my brother, he's all alone,
He's pointing pikes on the grinding stone.

'Twas in old Ireland this young man died,
And in old Ireland his body's laid,
All the good people that do pass by,
Pray the Lord have mercy on the Croppy Boy.

OLD MAID IN THE GARRET

G
I was told by my aunt,

I was told by my mother,

D
That going to a wedding

        G
Would soon bring another.

       C
Then, if that be so, sure,

G
I'd go without a bidding,

Oh, kind providence,

Won't you set me to a wedding.

CHORUS:

       C   G   C
And it's Oh dear me, how will it be,

    G   D   G
If I die an old maid in the garret?

Now there's me sister Jean,
She's not handsome or good-looking,
Scarcely sixteen
And a feller she was courtin'
Now she's twenty-four
With a son and a daughter,
Here I am forty-five
And I never had an offer.
REPEAT CHORUS

I can cook, I can sew,
I can keep the house quite tidy,
Rise up in the morning
And get the breakfast ready.
There's nothing in this whole world
That makes my heart so cheery,
As a wee fat man,
Who'd call me 'his own deary'.
REPEAT CHORUS

So come landsman, come townsman,
Come tinker and come tailor,
Come fiddler, come dancer,
Come ploughman and come sailor,
Come rich man, come poor man,
Come fool man, come witty,
Come any man at all
That will marry out of pity.
REPEAT CHORUS

TEDDY O'NEALE

G
I've come to the cabin

       C   D
He danced his wild jigs in,

   G
As neat a mud palace

          D
As ever was seen,

G
And consid'ring it served

   C   D
To keep poultry and pigs in,

   G
I'm sure it was always

      D   G
Most elegant clean!

Am
But now all about it

                 G
Seems lonely and dreary,

   Em
All sad and silent,

   C   D
No piper, no reel!

G
Not even the sun thro'

        C   D
The casement is cheery,

     G
Since I miss the dear darling boy,

D   G
Teddy O'Neale.

I dreamt but last night
(Oh! bad luck to my dreaming,
I'd die if I thought
'Twould come surely to pass.)
But I dreamt, while the tears
Down my pillow were coursing
That Teddy was courtin'
Another fair lass.
Och! did not I wake
With a weeping and wailing,
The grief of that thought
Was too deep to conceal;
My mother cried 'Norah, child,
What is your ailing?'
And all I could utter was
'Teddy O'Neale'.

Priests at play, 1933

THE GLENDALOUGH SAINT

D
In Glendalough lived an old saint,
      A
Renowned for his learning and piety.
 D   G
His manners were curious and quaint,
  D   A   D
And he looked upon girls with disparity.

CHORUS:
Ri fol di dol, fol di dol day,
Ri fol di dol, fol di dol laddy,
Ri fol di dol, fol di dol day,
Ri fol di dol, fol di dol laddy.

But as he was fishin' one day,
A-catchin' some kind of trout, sir,
Young Kathleen
Was walkin' that way
Just to see what the saint
Was about, sir.
'You're a mighty fine fisher',
Says Kate,
'Tis yourself is the boy
That can hook them,
But when you have
Caught them so nate,
Don't you want some young
Woman to cook them?'
REPEAT CHORUS

'Be gone out of that', said the saint,
'For I am a man of great piety,
Me character I wouldn't taint,
By keeping such class of society.'
But Kathleen wasn't goin' to give in,
For when he got home to his rockery,
He found her sitting therein,
A-polishing up of his crockery.
REPEAT CHORUS

He gave the poor creature a shake,
Oh, I wish that the peelers
Had caught him;
He threw her right into the lake,
And of course she sank
Down to the bottom.
It is rumoured from that very day,
Kathleen's ghost can be
Seen on the river;
And the saint never
Raised up his hand,
For he died of the right
Kind of fervour.
REPEAT CHORUS

LET HIM GO, LET HIM TARRY

G
Farewell to cold winter,
C   G
Summer's come at last
D
Nothing have I gained
        G
But my true-love I have lost,

I'll sing and I'll be happy
   C   G
Like the birds upon the tree,
 D
But since he deceived me
     G
I care no more for he.

CHORUS:
Let him go, let him tarry,
Let him sink or let him swim,
He doesn't care for me
Nor I don't care for him.
He can go and get another
And I hope he will enjoy,
For I'm going to marry
A far nicer boy.

He wrote me a letter
Saying he was very bad,
I sent him back an answer
Saying I was awful glad,
He wrote to me another
Saying he was was well and strong,
But I care no more about him
Than the ground he walks upon.
REPEAT CHORUS

Some of his friends
Had a good kind wish for me,
Others of his friends
They could hang me on a tree,
But soon I'll let them see my love,
And soon I'll let them know,
That I can get a new sweetheart
On any grounds I go.
REPEAT CHORUS

He can go to his old mother now
And set her mind at ease,
I hear she is an old, old woman,
Very hard to please,
It's slighting me and talking ill
Is what she's always done,
Because that I was courting
Her great big ugly son.
REPEAT CHORUS

HIGHLAND PADDY

G
One evening fair as the sun was shining,

To Kilkenny I did ride,
C G
I did meet with Captain Brady,
   D
A tall commander by his side.
        G
Then you are welcome, Highland Paddy,

By my side you'll surely stand,
C   G
Hear the people shout for freedom,
       D
We'll rise in the morning with the Fenian band,

Rise in the morning with the Fenian band.

In the mornin' we rose early,
Just before the break of dawn,
Blackbirds singing in the bushes,
Greetings to a smiling morn.
Gather 'round me men of Ireland,
Gather Fenians gather round,
Hand to hand with sword and musket,
Spill the blood upon this holy ground.
REPEAT CHORUS

There's a glen beside the river,
Just outside Kilkenny town,
There we met this noble captain,
Men lay dead upon the ground.
REPEAT CHORUS

There's a grave beside the river,
A mile outside Kilkenny town,
There we laid our noble captain,
Birds were silent when this Fenian died.
All my life I will remember
I'll remember night and day,
That once I rode into Kilkenny
And I heard this noble captain say.
REPEAT CHORUS

THE STREETS OF NEW YORK

G   C   G
I was eighteen years old, when I went down to Dublin

                                 D
With a fistful of money and a cartload of dreams

         G   D
'Take your time', said me father, 'stop rushing like hell,

        G   D   G
And remember all is not what it seems to be.

D   C   G
For there's fellows would cut you for the coat on your back,

                            D
Or the watch that you got from your mother.

     G   C   G   D
So take care me young bucko and mind yourself well

             G   D   G
And will you give this wee note to me brother'.

At the time Uncle Benjy was a p'liceman in Brooklyn
And me father the youngest looked after the farm.
When a phone call from America said 'send the lad over'
And the old fella said sure it wouldn't do any harm.
'For I spent my life working this dirty old ground
For a few pints of porter and the smell of a pound.
And sure maybe there's something you'll learn or you'll see,
And you can bring it back home, make it easy on me.'

So I landed at Kennedy and a big yellow taxi,
Carried me and my bags through the streets and the rain.
Well my poor heart was pumping around with excitement,
And I hardly even heard what the driver was saying.
We came in the short parkway to the flatlands in Brooklyn,
To my uncle's apartment on East 53rd,
I was feeling so happy I was humming a song,
And I sang 'you're as free as a bird'.

Well to shorten the story what I found out that day,
Was that Benjy got shot in a downtown foray,
And while I was flying my way to New York,
Poor Benjy was lying in a cold city morgue.
Well I phoned up the old fella, told him the news,
I could tell he could hardly stand up in his shoes.
And he wept as he told me, go ahead with the plan,
And not to forget to be a proud Irishman.

So I went up to Nelly's beside Fordham road,
And I started to learn about lifting the load,
But the healthiest thing that I carried that year,
Was the bitter sweet thoughts of my home town so dear.
I went home that December 'cause the old fella died,
Had to borrow the money from Phil on the side,
And all the bright flowers and grass couldn't hide,,
The poor wasted face of my father.

I sold up the old farmyard for what it was worth,
And into my bag stuck a handful of earth,
Then I boarded a train and I caught me a plane,
And I found myself back in the U.S. again.
It's been twenty-two years since I set foot in Dublin,
The kids know how to use the correct knife and fork,
But I'll never forget the green grass and the rivers,
As I keep law and order in the streets of New York.

MY SINGING BIRD

G
I have seen the lark soar

C   D
high at morn

     G   D
To sing up in the blue,

         G
I have heard the blackbird

C   D
pipe its song,

     G   D
The thrush and linnet too.

     G   C
But none of them can

Am
sing so sweet,

      D
My singing bird as you,

G   C   D
Aah . . . .

     G   D
My singing bird as you.

If I could lure my singing
bird
From its own cosy nest,
If I could catch my singing
bird
I would warm it on my
breast,
And on my heart my
singing bird
Would sing itself to rest,
Aah . . . .
Would sing itself to rest.

11

GOODBYE MICK

D
This ship it sails in half an hour,
A
To cross the broad Atlantic,

My friends are standing on the quay,
D
With grief and sorrow frantic,

I'm just about to sail away
A
In the good ship Don O'Leary,

The anchor's weighed and the gangway's up,
D
I'm leaving Tipperary.

CHORUS:
And it's goodbye Mick and goodbye Pat
And goodbye Kaye and Mary,
The anchor's weighed and the gangway's up,
I'm leaving Tipperary.
And now the steam is blowing off
I have no more to say,
I'm bound for New York City boys,
Three thousand miles away.

In my portmanteau here I have
Some cabbage beans and bacon,
And if yez think I can't eat that
Well there's where you're mistaken.
For this ship will play with pitch and toss
For half a dozen farthings,
I'll roll me bundle on me back
And walk to castle gardens.

Now I won't come that Yankee chat
I guess I'm calculatin'
Come liquor up old sonny boy
When an old friend I am treatin'.
I'm deep in love with Molly Burke
Like an ass is fond of clover,
I'll send for her when I get there,
That's if she will come over.
REPEAT CHORUS

Then fare thee well old Erin dear
To part me heart does ache well,
From Carrickfergus to Cape Clear
You'll never see your equal.
Although to foreign parts we're bound
Where cannibals may eat us
We'll ne'er forget the holy ground
Of Poteen and potatoes.
REPEAT CHORUS

When good St. Paddy banished snakes
He shook them from his garment
He never thought we'd go abroad
To look upon such vermint.
Nor quit this land where whiskey grew
To where the Yankee button
Take vinegar for mountain dew
And toads for mountain mutton.

SALLY GARDENS

G   C   G
Down by the Sally gardens,
D   G
My love and I did meet,
C   G
She passed the Sally gardens,
D   G
With little snow-white feet.
C   D
She bid me 'Take love easy,
C
As the leaves grow on the tree',
D   C G
But I, being young and foolish,
D   G
With her did not agree.

In a field down by the river,
My love and I did stand
And on my leaning shoulder,
She laid her snow-white hand.
She bid me take life easy,
As the grass grows on the weirs;
But I was young and foolish
And now am full of tears.

Goodbye to the emigrants,Queenstown, Cobh, Co. Cork, 1934

EASY AND SLOW

D   A
'Twas down by Christchurch
D
That I first met with Annie,

A neat little girl
       G   D
And not a bit shy,
D
She told me her father,
          G   D
Who came from Dungannon,

Would take her back home
       A   D
In the sweet by and by.

CHORUS:
G
And what's it to any man
           D
Whether or no,
G
Whether I'm easy or
D   A
Whether I'm true,
     G
As I lifted her petticoat
         D
Easy and slow,

And I tied up my sleeves
       G   · D
For to buckle her shoe.

And what's it to any man
Whether or no,
Whether I'm easy or
Whether I'm true,
As I lifted her petticoat
Easy and slow,
And I tied up my sleeves
For to buckle her shoe.

We wandered by Thomas Street
Down to the Liffey
The sunshine was gone
And the evening grew dark
Along by Kingsbridge
And begod in a jiffy
Me arms were around
Her beyond in the park.
REPEAT CHORUS

From city or county
A girl is a jewel
And well made for gripping
The most of them are
But any young man
He is really a fool
If he tries at the first time
To go a bit far.
REPEAT CHORUS

Now if you should go
To the town of Dungannon
You can search till your eyes
Are weary or blind
Be you lying or walking
Or sitting or running
A girl like Annie,
You never will find.
REPEAT CHORUS

THE LEAVING OF LIVERPOOL

D   G   D
Farewell to Princes' landing stage,
                   A
River Mersey fare thee well,
       D   G   D
I am bound for Californiay,
        A   D
A place I know right well.

CHORUS:
       A   G   D
So fare thee well, my own true love,
                      A
When I return united we will be,
         D   G   D
Its not the leaving of Liverpool that grieves me,
          A   D
But my darling when I think of thee.

I have shipped on a Yankee sailing ship,
Davy Crockett is her name,
And Burgess is the captain of her,
And they say that she's a floating shame.
REPEAT CHORUS

Oh the sun is on the harbour love,
And I wish I could remain,
For I know it will be a long, long time,
Before I see you again.
REPEAT CHORUS

14

THREE DRUNKEN MAIDENS

```
G                      C              D                   G
There were three drunken maidens came down from the Isle of Wight,
                        C               D                   G
They started to drink on Monday, never stopped till Saturday night.
    Am                                 G                    D
On Saturday night they came my lads but still they wouldn't get out,
    G                  C             D                  G
And then three drunken maidens did push the jug about.
```

Then in came dancing Sally
Her cheeks a rosy bloom,
Shove o'er you jolly sisters
And give young Sal some room,
And I will be your equal
Before the evening's out,
And then three drunken
maidens
They pushed the jug about.

They had woodcock and
pheasant,
Partridge and hare,
And every sort of dainty,
No shortage there was there.
They'd forty gallons of beer,
me lads
But still they wouldn't get out,
And then three drunken
maidens
They pushed the jug about.

Then in came the landlord,
He was looking for his pay,
Forty pounds for beer me lads
These girls were forced to pay,
They had ten pounds a piece,
me lads
But still they wouldn't get out,
And then three drunken
maidens
They pushed the jug about.

Where are your fancy hats
And your mantles rich and fine,
They've all been swallowed up,
me lads
With tankards of fine wine.
And where are your fancy men,
Young maidens frisk and gay,
You left them in the ale house
And it's there you'll have to pay.

Mackerel Fishing at Cobh, 1941

I KNOW MY LOVE

```
D        A       D                    A                  D
I know my love by his way of walking and I know my love by his way of talking,
      A               D                    A                 D
And I know my love by his suit of blue, but if my love leaves me, what will I do?
```

CHORUS:
```
      A                 D                    A                D
And yet she cries 'I love him the best' but a troubled mind sure can know no rest.
      A               D                    A                 D
And yet she cries 'Bonny boys are few', yet if my love leaves me, what will I do?
```

There is a dance house in Mardyke, and 'tis there my dear love goes every night:
And he takes a strange girl all on his knee, and don't you think but it troubles me.
REPEAT CHORUS

If my love knew I could wash and wring, and if my love knew I could weave and spin,
I could make a suit all of the finest kind, but the want of money, it leaves me behind.
REPEAT CHORUS

NOVA SCOTIA

CHORUS:

G
Oh farewell to Nova Scotia the sea-bound coast,

Em
Let your mountains dark and dear I be,

G   D
Oh when I'm far away o'er the grimy ocean tossed,

Em
Will you ever hear a sigh or a wish for me.

I grieve to leave my native land,
I grieve to leave my comrades all,
And my parents whom I held so dear,
And the bonny bonny lassie that I do adore.
REPEAT CHORUS

The drums do beat and the wars do alarm,
And the captain's call we must obey.
So farewell, farewell, to Nova Scotia's charms,
For it's early in the morning I'll be far far away.
REPEAT CHORUS

I have three Brothers and they are at rest,
And their arms are folded on their breast,
But a poor simple sailor just like me,
Must be tossed and driven on the dark blue sea.
REPEAT CHORUS

THE SNOWY-BREASTED PEARL

D   G   D
There's a colleen fair as May

A
For a year and for a day,

D   G
I have sought by ev'ry way

A   D
Her heart to gain.

There's no art of tongue or eye.
Fond youths with maidens try,
But I've tried with ceaseless sigh,
Yet tried in vain.

D   Em   A
If to France or far-off Spain

G   D
She'd cross the wat'ry main.

A
To see her face again

The seas I'd brave.

D
And if 'tis heav'ns decree

A
That mine she may not be.

D   G
May the Son of Mary me

A   D
In mercy save.

Oh, thou blooming milk-white dove
To whom I've given my love,
Do not ever thus reprove
My constancy.

There are maidens would be mine
With wealth in land and kine,
If my heart would but incline
To turn from thee.

But a kiss with welcome bland
And touch of thy fair hand,
Is all that I demand,
Would'st thou not spurn.

For if not mine, dear girl,
Oh, snowy-breasted pearl,
May I never from the fair
With life return.

THE WELL
BELOW THE VALLEY

Em
A gentleman was passing by,
D
He asked a drink as he got dry,
Em   D   Em
At this well below the valley-o.

CHORUS:

D Em
Green grows the lily-o,
D   Em
Right among the bushes-o.

She said 'my cup it overflows,
If I stoop down I might fall in,'
At the well below the valley-o.

If your true love was passing by,
You'd fill him a drink if he got dry
At the well below the valley-o.

She swore by grass, she swore by corn,
That her true love was never born,
At the well below the valley-o.

I say, young maid, you're swearing wrong,
For five fine children you had born
At the well below the valley-o.

If you're a man of noble fame,
You'll tell me who's the father of them,
At the well below the valley-o.

There was two of them by your uncle Dan,
Another two by your brother John,
At the well below the valley-o.

Another by your father dear
At the well below the valley-o,
At the well below the valley-o.

Well if you're a man of noble fame,
You'll tell me what did happen to them,
At the well below the valley-o.

There was two of them buried by the stable door,
Another two 'neath the kitchen floor,
At the well below the valley-o.

Another's buried by the well,
At the well below the valley-o,
At the well below the valley-o.

Well if you're a man of noble fame,
You'll tell me what will happen myself
At the well below the valley-o.

You'll be seven years a-porterin in hell,
And seven years a-ringing a bell,
At the well below the valley-o.

I'll be seven years a-ringing a bell
But the Lord above may save my soul from portin' in hell,
At the well below the valley-o.

THE HOLY GROUND

D   A   D
Adieu, my fair young maiden,
A   D
A thousand times adieu.
G
We must bid farewell to the Holy Ground
D   A
And the girls that we love true.
D   A   D
We will sail the salt sea over,
A
And return again for sure,
D
To seek the girls who wait for us
A   D
In the Holy Ground once more.

CHORUS:

FINE GIRL YOU ARE

D   A
You're the girl that I adore,
D
And still I live in hopes to see
A   D
The Holy Ground once more.

FINE GIRL YOU ARE

Oh the night was dark and stormy,
You scarce could see the moon,
And our good old ship was tossed about,
And her rigging was all torn;
With her seams agape and leaky,
With her timbers dozed and old,
And still I live in hopes to see
The Holy Ground once more
REPEAT CHORUS

19

SONNY'S DREAM

D
'Sonny, don't go away,

I'm here all alone,

Your daddy's a sailor,
G   D
Never comes home.
A
Nights are so long,

Silence goes on,
G   D
I'm feelin' so tired
          A
And not all that strong.'

Sonny lives on a farm
In a wide open space,
'Take off your shoes,
Son, stay out of the race,
Lay down your head
By the soft river bed.'
Sonny always remembers
The words his mammy said.

Sonny works on the land
Though he's barely a man
There's not much to do,
He just does what he can.
He sits at the window
Of his room by the stairs,
He watches the waves
Gently wash on the pier.

Many years have passed on,
Sonny's old and alone,
His daddy the sailor
Never came home.
Sometimes he wonders
What his life might have been
But from the grave mammy
Still haunts his dreams.

Children playing hopscotch, Galway 1939

THE ROCKY ROAD TO DUBLIN

Em
In the merry month of May

From my home I started,

Left the girls of Tuam
D
Nearly broken-hearted,
Em
Saluted father dear,

Kissed my darlin' mother,

Drank a pint of beer,
D
My grief and tears to smother,
Em   D
Then off to reap the corn
Em   D
And leave where I was born,
Em
I cut a stout blackthorn,
D
To banish ghost and goblin,
Em
In a bran' new pair of brogues

I rattled o'er the bogs
              D
And frightened all the dogs

On the rocky road to Dublin

CHORUS:
Em
One, two, three, four, five,

Hunt the hare and turn her
D
Down the rocky road

And all the ways to Dublin,
Em
Whack fol lol de ra.

In Mullingar that night
I rested limbs so weary,
Started by daylight
Next morning light and airy,
Took a drop of the pure,
To keep my heart from sinking,
That's an Irishman's cure,
Whene'er he's on for drinking,
To see the lasses smile,
Laughing all the while,
At my curious style,
'Twould set your heart a-bubbling,

They ax'd if I was hired,
The wages I required,
Till I was almost tired
Of the rocky road to Dublin.
REPEAT CHORUS

In Dublin next arrived,
I thought it such a pity,
To be so soon deprived
A view of that fine city,
Then I took a stroll
Among the quality,
My bundle it was stole
In a neat locality;
Something crossed my mind,
Then I looked behind,
No bundle could I find
Upon me stick a-wobblin',
Enquiring for the rogue,
They said my Connaught brogue,
Wasn't much in vogue
On the rocky road to Dublin.
REPEAT CHORUS

From there I got away
My spirits never failing,
Landed on the quay
As the ship was sailing,
Captain at me roared,
Said that no room had he,
When I jumped aboard,
A cabin found for Paddy,
Down among the pigs,
I played some funny rigs,
Danced some hearty jigs,
The water round me bubblin'
When off to Holyhead
I wished myself was dead,
Or better far, instead,
On the rocky road to Dublin.
REPEAT CHORUS

The boys of Liverpool,
When we safely landed,
Called myself a fool,
I could no longer stand it;
Blood began to boil,
Temper I was losin'
Poor old Erin's isle
They began abusin'
'Hurrah my soul,' sez I,
My shillelagh I let fly,
Some Galway boys were by,
Saw I was a hobble in,
Then with a loud Hurrah,
They joined in the affray,
We quickly cleared the way
For the rocky road to Dublin.
REPEAT CHORUS

THE GYPSY

D
Do you think that you're in love with me,
    A
Will you listen to what I say,

You're too young to come with me girl,
  D
I'll soon be on my way.

Stop your silly crying now,
              G
How can I make you see,
          D
That I'm a gypsy rover, love,
    A   D
And you can't come with me.

    G   A   D
Go home, girl, go home.

You met me at the market
When your Ma was not with you,
And you liked my long brown ringlets,
And my handkerchief of blue.
Although I'm very fond of you
And you asked me home to tea,
I am a gypsy rover, love,
And you can't come with me.

Go home, girl, go home.

Your brother is a peeler
And he would put me in jail,
If he knew I was a poacher
And I hunt your lord's best game.
Your Daddy is a gentleman,
Your Mammy is just as grand,
But I'm a gypsy rover, love,
I'll not be your husband.

Go home, girl, go home.

The hour's drawing on, love,
And your Ma's expecting thee,
Don't you tell her that you met me here,
Or I'm a gypsy.
Let's get off my jacket now,
Your love will have to wait,
For I am twenty-two years old,
And you you're only eight.

Go home, girl, go home.
Go home, girl, go home.

THE CASTLE OF DROMORE

G   C
October winds lament
  G
Around the castle of Dromore,

Yet peace is in its lofty halls,
    C   D   G
A phaisde bán a stór.
              C   D   C   G
Though Autumn winds may droop and die
          C   G
A bud of spring are you,
      C
Sing hushabye,
D   G
Lul, lul, lo, lo, lan,
        C
Sing hushabye,
D   G
Lul, lul, loo.

Bring no ill wind to hinder us,
My helpless babe and me -
Dread spirit of Blackwater banks,
Clan Eoin's wild banshee,
And Holy Mary pitying,
In heaven for grace doth sue,
Sing hushabye,
Lul, lul, lo, lo, lan,
Sing hushabye,
Lul, lul, loo.

Take time to thrive, my Rose of hope,
In the garden of Dromore;
Take heed young Eagle - till your wings
Are weathered fit to soar;
A little time and then our land
Is full of things to do,
Sing hushabye,
Lul, lul, lo, lo, lan,
Sing hushabye,
Lul, lul, loo.

WEILE WAILE

D   G D
Well there was an old woman and she lived in the woods, weile weile waile.
  A   D
There was an old woman and she lived in the woods, down by the river Saile.

She had a baby three months old, weile weile waile.
She had a baby three months old, down by the river Saile.

She had a penknife long and sharp, weile weile waile.
She had a penknife long and sharp, down by the river Saile.

She stuck the pen-knife in the baby's heart, weile weile waile.
She stuck the pen-knife in the baby's heart, down by the river Saile.

Three policemen came knocking at the door, weile weile waile.
Three policemen came knocking at the door, down by the river Saile.

Are you the woman that killed the child, weile weile waile.
Are you the woman that killed the child, down by the river Saile.

The rope was pulled and she was hung, weile weile waile.
The rope was pulled and she was hung, down by the river Saile.

And that was the end of the woman in the woods, weile weile waile.
And that was the end of the baby too, down by the river Saile.

Two little kids, Dunamase, Co. Laois, 1940

MAIDS WHEN YOU'RE YOUNG

```
G                              D
An old man came courting me, hey ding a doorum dah
G                              D
An old man came courting me, me being young.
    G          C        G      C
An old man came courting me, all for his wife to be,
G              C          D        G ,
Maids when you're young never wed an old man.
```

CHORUS:
For he's got no faloo doo rum, fal diddle oo doo rum,
He's got no faloo doo rum, fal diddle day.
He's got no faloo doo rum, lost his ding doo reeum,
Maids when you're young never wed an old man.

When this old man comes to bed, hey ding a doorum dah
When this old man comes to bed, me being young.
When this old man comes to bed, he lays like a lump of lead,
Maids when you're young never wed an old man.
REPEAT CHORUS

When this old man goes to sleep, hey ding a doorum dah
When this old man goes to sleep, me being young.
When this old man goes to sleep, out of bed I do creep,
Into the arms of a handsome young man.
REPEAT CHORUS

I wish this old man would die, hey ding a doorum dah
I wish this old man would die, me being young.
I wish this old man would die, I'd make the money fly,
Girls for your sakes never wed an old man.
REPEAT CHORUS

A young man is my delight, hey ding a doorum dah
A young man is my delight, me being young.
A young man is my delight, he'll kiss you day and night,
Maids when you're young never wed an old man.
REPEAT CHORUS

QUARE BUNGLE RYE

G
Now Jack was a sailor

Who roamed on the town,

    C   G
And she was a damsel

          D
Who skipped up and down,

  G
Said the damsel to Jack

As she passed him by,

      C   G
'Would you care for to purchase

  C   G   D
Some quare bungle rye, roddy rye?

               G
Fol the diddle rye roddy rye roddy rye.'

Thought Jack to himself
'Now what can this be,
But the finest of whiskey
From far Germany,
Smuggled up in a basket
And sold on the sly,
And the name that it goes by
Is quare bungle rye, roddy rye,' etc.

Jack gave her a pound
And he thought nothing strange,
Said she 'Hold the basket
Till I get you your change.'
Jack looked in the basket
And a baby did spy,
'Oh Begorrah,' says Jack,
'This is a quare bungle rye, roddy rye,' etc.

Now to get the child christened
Was Jack's first intent,
For to get the child christened
To the parson he went.
Says the parson to Jack,
'What will he go by?'
'Bedad, now,' says Jack,
'Call him quare bungle rye, roddy rye,' etc.

Says the parson to Jack,
'Now that's a queer name,'
Says Jack to the parson,
'It's a queer way he came,
Smuggled up in a basket
And sold on the sly,
And the name that he'll go by
Is Quare Bungle Rye, Roddy Rye,' etc.

Now all you young sailors
Who roam on the town,
Beware of those damsels
Who skip up and down,
Take a look in their baskets
As they pass you by,
Or else they might sell you
Some quare bungle rye, roddy rye, etc.

DOWN BY THE GLENSIDE

Em   G
'Twas down by the glenside
Em   G
I met an old woman,
  Em   G
A-plucking young nettles
    Em   G
Nor saw I was coming,
  Em   C
I listened a while to the song
          D
She was humming,
Em   G
Glory-o, Glory-o,
        Em
To the Bold Fenian Men.

'Tis sixteen long years
Since I saw the moon beaming,
On brave manly forms
And their eyes were heart gleaming,
I see them all now sure
In all my day-dreaming,
Glory-o, Glory-o,
To the Bold Fenian Men.

Some died on the hillside,
Some died with a stranger,
And wise men have judged
That their cause was a failure,
They fought for old Ireland
And they never feared danger,
Glory-o, Glory-o,
To the Bold Fenian Men.

I passed on my way,
Thanks to God that I met her,
Be life long or short,
Sure I'll never forget her,
There may have been brave men,
But they'll never be better,
Glory-o, Glory-o,
To the Bold Fenian Men.

WILL YOU COME TO THE BOWER?

D   A
Will you come to the bow'r
D
O'er the free boundless ocean,
         A
Where the stupendous waves
       D
Roll in thundering motion,

Where the mermaids are seen
      A
And the fierce tempest gathers,
    D
To loved Erin the green,
   A
The dear land of our fathers.

CHORUS:
     D   A
Will you come, will you, will you,
      D
Will you come to the bower.

Will you come to the land
Of O'Neill and O'Donnell,
Of Lord Lucan of old
And the immortal O'Connell.
Where Brian drove the Danes
And St. Patrick the vermin,
And whose valleys remain
Still most beautiful and charming
REPEAT CHORUS

You can visit Benburb
And the storied Blackwater,
Where Owen Roe met Munroe
And his chieftains did slaughter
Where the lambs skip and play
On the mossey all over
From those golden bright views
To enchanting Rostrevor.
REPEAT CHORUS

You can see Dublin city
And the fine groves of Blarney,
The Bann, the Boyne, the Liffey
And the lakes of Killarney;
You may ride on the tide
O'er the broad majestic Shannon,
You may sail round Lough Neagh
And see storied Dungannon.
REPEAT CHORUS

You can visit New Ross,
Gallant Wexford and Gorey,
Where the green grass was last seen
By proud Saxon and Tory,
Where the soil is sanctified
By the blood of each true man,
Where they died satisfied,
Their enemies they would not run from.
REPEAT CHORUS

Will you come and awake
Our lost land from its slumber,
And her fetters we will break,
Links that long are encumbered
And the air will resound
With Hosanna to greet you,
On the shore will be found
Gallant Irishmen to meet you.
REPEAT CHORUS

THE HILLS OF CONNEMARA

D   G   D
Gather up the pots and the old tin can,
                  A
The mash, the corn, the barley and the bran,
D   G   D
Run like the devil from the excise man,
                  A   D
Keep the smoke from rising, Barney.

Keep your eyes well peeled today,
The tall, tall men are on their way,
Searching for the mountain tay,
In the Hills of Connemara.

Swing to the left and swing to the right,
The excise men will dance all night,
Drinking up the tay till the broad
daylight,
In the Hills of Connemara.

A gallon for the butcher, a quart for Tom,
A bottle for poor old Father Tom,
To help the poor old dear along,
In the Hills of Connemara.

Stand your ground, it is too late,
The excise men are at the gate,
Glory be to Paddy, but they're drinking it
nate,
In the Hills of Connemara.

The Spinning Wheel, Cloone, Co. Leitrim, 1933

SPINNINGWHEEL SONG

D   A
Mellow, the moonlight to shine is beginning,
                  G   D
Close by the window young Eileen is spinning,
                  G   D
Bent o'er the fire, her blind grandmother sitting,
G   D   A   D
Crooning and moaning and drowsily knitting.

CHORUS:
D   A
Merrily, cheerily, noiselessly whirring,
                              D
Spins the wheel, rings the wheel, while the foot's stirring.
                 G   D
Lightly and brightly and airily ringing,
G   D   A   D
Sounds the sweet voice of the young maiden singing.

What's the noise that I hear at the window I wonder,
'Tis the little birds chirping the holly-bush under'
'What makes you be shoving and moving your stool on,
An' singing, all wrong, that old song of "The Coolun"?'

There's a form at the casement - the form of her true love,
And he whispers, with face bent: 'I'm waiting for you, love,
Get up from the stool, through the lattice step lightly,
We'll rove in the grove while the moon's shining brightly.'

CHORUS:
Merrily, cheerily, noiselessly whirring,
Spins the wheel, rings the wheel, while the foot's stirring.
Sprightly and lightly and airily ringing,
Trills the sweet voice of the young maiden singing.

The maid shakes her head, on her lip lays her fingers,
Steals up from the stool - longs to go and yet lingers.
A frightened glance turns to her drowsy grandmother,
Puts one foot on the stool, spins the wheel with the other.

CHORUS:
Lazily, easily, swings now the wheel round,
Slowly and lowly is heard now the reel's sound,
Noiseless and light to the lattice above her,
The maid steps - then leaps to the arms of her lover.

CHORUS:
Slower - and slower - and slower the wheel swings
Lower - and lower - and lower the reel rings;
Ere the reel and the wheel stop their ringing and moving,
Through the grove the young lovers by moonlight are roving.

CONNEMARA CRADLE SONG

D
On wings of the wind,
                    A
O'er the dark rolling deep,

Angels are coming to
                 D
Watch o'er thy sleep,

Angels are coming
              A
To watch over thee,

So list to the wind
G   D
Coming over the sea.

CHORUS:
Hear the wind blow love,
Hear the wind blow,
Lean your head over,
And hear the wind blow.

Oh, winds of the night,
May your fury be crossed,
May no one that's dear
To our island be lost,
Blow the wind lightly,
Calm be the foam,
Shine the light brightly
To guide them home.
REPEAT CHORUS

The Currachs are sailing
Way out in the blue,
Laden with herrin'
Of silvery hue,
Silver the herrin'
And silver the sea,
And soon they'll be silver
For baby and me.
REPEAT CHORUS

The Currachs tomorrow
Will stand on the shore,
And daddy goes sailing,
A-sailing no more,
The nets will be drying,
The nets heaven blessed,
And safe in my arms dear,
Contented he'll rest.
REPEAT CHORUS

OLD WOMAN FROM WEXFORD

D
There was an old woman from Wexford,

A   D
In Wexford she did dwell,

           G
She loved her husband dearly,

A   G
But another man twice as well.

CHORUS:

      D
With me rum a dum dum a dero,

A   D
And me dum a dero dee.

One day she went to the doctor,
Some medicine for to find,
She said 'Will you give me something,
That will make my old man blind.'
REPEAT CHORUS

'Feed him eggs and marrow bones
And make him suck them all,
And it won't be very long after,
Till he won't see you at all.'
REPEAT CHORUS

The doctor wrote a letter
And he signed it with his hand,
And he sent it to the old man,
Just to make him understand.
REPEAT CHORUS

So she fed him eggs and marrow bones
And made him suck them all,
And it wasn't very long after
Till he couldn't see the wall.
REPEAT CHORUS

He said 'I'll go and drown myself
But I fear it is a sin,'
Says she, 'I'll go along with you
And help to push you in.'
REPEAT CHORUS

The woman she stepped back a bit
To rush and push him in,
But the old man quietly stepped aside
And she went tumbling in.
REPEAT CHORUS

Oh how loudly she did yell
And how loudly she did call,
'Yerra, hold your whist,
Old woman,' says he.
REPEAT CHORUS

So eggs are eggs and marrow bones
May make your old man blind,
But if you want to drown him,
You must creep up close behind.
REPEAT CHORUS

THE CLIFFS OF DOONEEN

G   D   G
You may travel far, far

            C   D
From your own native home,

     G
Far away o'er the mountains,

     D   G
Far away o'er the foam,

But of all the fine places

     D   Em
That I've ever been,

        G
Oh, there's none can compare

         C   D
With the Cliffs of Dooneen.

It's a nice place to be
On a fine summer's day,
Watching all the wild flowers
That ne'er do decay,
Oh, the hare and the pheasant
Are plain to be seen,
Making homes for their young
Round the Cliffs of Dooneen.

Take a view o'er the mountains,
Fine sights you'll see there;
You'll see the high rocky mountains
On the west coast of Clare,
Oh, the towns of Kilkee
And Kilrush can be seen,
From the high rocky slopes
Round the Cliffs of Dooneen.

So fare thee well to Dooneen,
Fare thee well for a while,
And although we are parted
By the raging sea wild,
Once again I will wander
With my Irish colleen,
Round the high rocky slopes
Of the Cliffs of Dooneen.

THE RISING OF THE MOON

D
Oh, then tell me Sean O'Farrell,

A
Tell me why you hurry so?

G   D
Hush, hush, me buchall, hush and listen

A   D
And his cheeks were all aglow,

I bear orders from the captain,

A
Get you ready quick and soon,

G   D
For the pikes must be together

A   D
By the rising of the moon.

CHORUS:

D
By the rising of the moon,

A
By the rising of the moon,

G   D
For the pikes must be together

A   D
By the rising of the moon.

Oh, then tell me Sean O'Farrell
Where the gathering is to be,
'In the old spot by the river,
Right well known to you and me.
One more word for signal token,
Whistle up the marching tune,
With your pike upon your shoulder,
By the rising of the moon.
REPEAT CHORUS

Out from many a mudwall cabin
Eyes were watching through the night,
Many a manly heart was throbbing
For the blessed warning light.
Murmurs passed along the valley
Like the banshee's lonely croon,
And a thousand blades were flashing
At the rising of the moon.
REPEAT CHORUS

There beside the singing river
That dark mass of men were seen,
Far above the shining weapons
Hung their own beloved green.
Death to every foe and traitor,
Forward strike the marching tune,
And, Hurrah, my boys for freedom,
'Tis the rising of the moon.
REPEAT CHORUS

Well they fought for poor old Ireland
And full bitter was their fate,
Oh what glorious pride and sorrow
Fills the name of ninety-eight.
Yet, thank God, while hearts are beating
In manhood's burning noon,
We will follow in the footsteps
Of the rising of the moon.
REPEAT CHORUS

LOVE IS PLEASING

D   A
I wish, I wish, I wish in vain,

D
I wish I was a youth again,

A
But a youth again I will never be,

D
Till apples grow on an ivy tree.

Oh, love is pleasin'
And love is teasin'
And love is a pleasure
When first it's new.
But as it grows older,
Sure the love grows colder,
And it fades away
Like the morning dew.

I left my father,
I left my mother,
I left all my brothers
And sisters too.
I left all my friends
And my own relations,
I left them all for to follow you.

But the sweetest apple
Is the soonest rotten,
And the heart of love
Is the soonest cold,
And what can't be cured love,
Has to be endured, love,
And now I am bound for America.

And love and porter
Make a young man older,
And love and whiskey
Make him old and grey.
And what can't be cured love,
Has to be endured, love,
And now I am bound for America.

IN DUBLIN'S FAIR CITY

```
G                                    Am
In Dublin's fair city, where the girls are so pretty,
   G                              D
I first set my eyes on sweet Molly Malone,
     G                              Am
She wheeled a wheel-barrow, through streets broad and narrow,
       G
Crying: 'Cockles and Mussels a-live, a-live oh.'
```

CHORUS:
```
G                    Am
A-live, a-live oh, a-live, a-live oh,
       G                          D   G
Crying: 'Cockles and Mussels a-live, a-live oh.'
```

She was a fishmonger, but sure 'twas no wonder,
For so were her father and mother before;
And they both wheeled their barrow, through streets broad and narrow,
Crying: 'Cockles and Mussels a-live, a-live oh.'
REPEAT CHORUS

She died of a fever, no one could relieve her
And that was the end of sweet Molly Malone,
But her ghost wheels her barrow, through streets broad and narrow,
Crying: 'Cockles and Mussels a-live, a-live oh.'
REPEAT CHORUS

ALSO AVAILABLE IN THIS SERIES:
Duncles 50 Great Irish Ballads Volume 2
Duncles 50 Great Irish Ballads Volume 3

Digging up O'Connell Street, Dublin with sledge hammer and chisel, 1930

MY LOVELY ROSE OF CLARE

CHORUS:

D
Oh my lovely rose of Clare,
        G   D
You're the sweetest girl I know,
       A
You're the Queen of all the roses
   D
Like the pretty flowers that grow,

You are the sunshine of my life
 G   D
So beautiful and fair,
 A
And I will always love you,
 G   D
My lovely Rose of Clare.

Oh the sun it shines out like a jewel,
On the lovely hills of Clare,
As I strolled along with my sweet lass,
One evening at the fair,
Her eyes they shone like silver streams,
Her long and golden hair,
For I have won the heart of one,
My lovely Rose of Clare.
REPEAT CHORUS

As we walked down by the river bank,
Watched the Shannon flowing by,
And listened to the nightingale,
Singing songs for you and I,
And to say farewell
To all you true and fair,
For I have stolen the heart of one,
My lovely Rose of Clare.
REPEAT CHORUS

THE GAY GALTEE MOUNTAINS

G
On the gay Galtee Mountains
C   G
So far away,

I will tell you a story
              Am
That happened one day,
G
It's about a fair maiden,

Her age was sixteen,
        Am   D
And she sported the colours,
        G
White, orange and green.

A young British soldier
Was passing that day,
And he spied the fair maiden
With colours so gay,
He rode along-side her,
Jumped from his machine,
And he tried for to capture
The flag of Sinn Fein.

You'll not get these colours,
The fair maiden said,
You'll not get these colours
Until I am dead,
I'll fight by the Glenside,
It remains to be seen,
And I'll die for my colours,
White, orange and green.

'Twas early next morning
In Tipperary town,
From the gay Galtee mountains
The young maiden came down,
She was sick in her heart,
It was plain to be seen,
For they murdered Tom Ashe
For the flag of Sinn Fein.

THE BEGGARMAN'S SONG

```
D                              G
I am a little beggarman and begging I have been,
      D                           C
For three score years in this little isle of green.
D                                    G
I'm known along the Liffey from the Basin to the Zoo,
      D
And ev'ry body calls me by the name of Johnny Dhu.
C
Of all trades a-going, sure the begging is the best,
D                                        C
For when a man is tired he can sit him down and rest.
D                                    G
He can beg for his dinner, he has nothing else to do,
      D
But to slip around the corner with his ould rigadoo.
```

I slept in a barn one night in Currabawn,
A shocking wet night it was but I slept until the dawn;
There was holes in the roof and the raindrops coming through,
And the rats and the cats were all playing peek-a-boo.
Who did I waken but the woman of the house,
With her white spotted apron and her fine gingham blouse;
She began to get excited and all I said was 'Boo!,
Sure don't be afraid at all, 'tis only Johnny Dhu.'

I met a little girl when a-walking out one day,
'Good morrow, little flaxen-haired girl', I did say;
'Good morrow, little beggarman, and how do you do,
With your rags and your tags and your ould rigadoo.'
'I'll buy a pair of leggings and a collar and a tie,
And a nice young lady I'll go courting by and by;
I'll buy a pair of goggles and I'll colour them with blue,
And an old-fashioned lady I will make her too.'

So all along the highroad with my bag upon my back,
Over the fields with my bulging heavy sack;
With holes in my shoes and my toes a-peeping through,
Singing 'Skin-a-ma-link-a-doodle with my old rigadoo,
Oh, I must be going to bed,for it's getting late at night,
The fire is all raked and and now 'tis out the light;
For now you've heard the story of my ould rigadoo,
So goodbye and God be with you, from old Johnny Dhu.

THE WILD ROVER

```
G
I've been a wild rover
                        C
For many's the year,
                G          D
And I've spent all me money
                G
On whiskey and beer.
```

But now I'm returning
                        C
With gold in great store,
      G   D
And I never will play
                G
The wild rover no more.

```
CHORUS:
            D
And it's No, Nay, Never,
G                      C
No, Nay, Never, No more,
      G              C
Will I play the wild rover,
      G      D  G
No, Never, No more.
```

I went to an alehouse
I used to frequent,
And I told the landlady
My money was spent.
I asked her for credit
She answered me 'Nay,
Such custom as yours
I could have every day.'
REPEAT CHORUS

I brought up from my pockets
Ten sovereigns bright
And the landlady's eyes
Opened wide with delight.
She said 'I have whiskeys
And wines of the best,
And the words that I told you
Were only in jest.'
REPEAT CHORUS

I'll go home to my parents,
Confess what I've done,
And I'll ask them to pardon
Their prodigal son.
And when they've caressed me
As oft times before,
I never will play
The wild rover no more.
REPEAT CHORUS

The Knife Grinder, Cobh, 1934

THE LOWLANDS OF HOLLAND

D   G   D
Last night I was a-married
        G   D
And in my wedding bed,
       A   D
Up came a bold sea-captain,
       A
And stood at my bed-head,
      D   G   D
Saying 'Arise, arise, young married man,
        G   A
And come along with me,
  D
To the lowlands of Holland
     A
For to fight the enemy.'

I held my love in my arms
Still thinking he might stay,
But the captain gave another shout;
He was forced to go away,
'Tis many a blithe young married man
This night must go with me,
To the Lowlands of Holland to fight the enemy.

Oh Holland it is a wondrous place
And in it grows much green,
It's too wild a habitation
For my true love to lie in,
The wild flowers grow most plenteous there
And fruit on every tree,
But the Lowlands of Holland
Are between my love and me.

They took my love to a gallant ship,
A ship of noble fame,
With four and twenty seamen bold
To sail across the main.
The storm then began to rise
And the seas began to shout,
'Twas then my love and his gallant ship
Were sorely tossed about.

Says the mother to the daughter
'What makes you so lament,
Is there ne'er a man in Ireland
Who will please your discontent?'
'There are men enough in Ireland
But none at all for me,
In the Lowlands of Holland,
My love is across the sea.'

I'll wear not shoe or stocking
Or a comb put in my hair
Nor fire bright nor candle light
Shall show my beauty rare,
Nor will I wed with any man
Until the day I die,
Since the Lowlands of Holland
Are between my love and me.

MARY FROM DUNGLOE

G   D   C   G
Oh, then fare ye well, sweet Donegal,
          C   G
The Rosses and Gweedore,
           D   C D
I'm crossing the main ocean,
       C   G
Where the foaming billows roar.
          D   C   D
It breaks my heart from you to part,
     C   G
Where I spent many happy days,
         D   C G
Farewell to kind relations,
        C   G
I'm bound for Amerikay.

Oh, my love is tall and handsome
And her age is scarce eighteen,
She far exceeds all other fair maids
When she trips o'er the green.
Her lovely neck and shoulders
Are fairer than the snow,
Till the day I die I'll ne'er deny
My Mary from Dungloe.

If I was at home in sweet Dungloe
A letter I would write,
Kind thoughts would fill my bosom
For Mary, my delight.
'Tis in her father's garden
The fairest violets grow,
And 'twas there I came to court the maid,
My Mary from Dungloe.

Ah, then Mary, you're my heart's delight
My pride and only care,
It was your cruel father
Would not let me stay there.
But absence makes the heart grow fonder
And when I'm o'er the main,
May the Lord protect my darling girl,
Till I return again.

And I wished I was in sweet Dungloe
And seated on the grass,
And by my side a bottle of wine
And on my knee a lass.
I'd call for liquor of the best
And I'd pay before I would go,
And I'd roll my Mary in my arms
In the town of sweet Dungloe.

ARTHUR MC BRIDE

```
G                                             C       G                    C
I had a first cousin called Arthur Mc Bride, he and I took a stroll down by the sea-side
   G                                           D          C  D
A-seeking good fortune and what might betide, 'twas just as the day was a-dawning.
      G           C       G       C        G          C
Then after resting we both took a tramp, we met Sergeant Harper and Corporal Cramp
   G                                       D                    G
Besides the wee drummer who beat up for camp, with his rowdy-dow-dow in the morning.
```

He says 'My young fellows, if you will enlist. a Guinea you quickly shall have in your fist
Besides a Crown for to kick up the dust, and drink the King's health in the morning.'
Had we been such fools as to take the advance, the wee bitter morning we had run to chance
For you'd think it no scruple to send us to France, where we would be killed in the morning

He says 'My young fellows, if I hear but one word, I instantly now will out with my sword
And into your bodies as strength will afford, so now, my gay devils take warning.'
But Arthur and I we took in the odds, we gave them no chance to lunge out their swords
Our whacking shillelaghs came over their heads, and paid them right smart in the morning.

As for the wee drummer; we rifled his pouch, and we made a football of his rowdy-dow-dow
And into the ocean to rock and to row, and bade him a tedious returning.
As for the old rapier that hung by his side, we flung it as far as we could in the tide,
'To the devil I bid you', says Arthur Mc Bride, to temper your steel in the morning.'

THE ROSE OF MOONCOIN

```
G                        C          G
How sweet 'tis to roam by the sunny Suir stream
   D                                    G
And hear the dove coo 'neath the morning sunbeam,
                                  C          G
Where the thrush and the robin their sweet notes entwine,
      D                                    G
On the banks of the Suir that flows down by Mooncoin.
```

CHORUS:

```
                        C     G
Flow on lovely river, flow gently along,
      D                                    G
By your waters so sweet sounds the lark's merry song.
                                  C       G
On your green banks I'll wander where first I did join,
      D                              G
With you lovely Molly, the Rose of Mooncoin.
```

Oh! Molly, dear Molly, it breaks my fond heart
To know that we two for ever must part.
I'll think of you, Molly, while sun and moon shine
On the banks of the Suir that flows down by Mooncoin.
REPEAT CHORUS

She has sailed far away o'er the dark rolling foam
Far away from the hills of her dear Irish home
Where the fisherman sports with his small boat and line
On the banks of the Suir that flows down by Mooncoin.
REPEAT CHORUS

Then here's to the Suir with its valleys so fair
As oft' times we wandered in the cool morning air
Where the roses are blooming and lilies entwine
On the banks of the Suir that flows down by Mooncoin.
REPEAT PCHORUS

PADDY LAY BACK

G   D
Oh it was a cold and dreary morning in the December,
                          G
And all of me money being spent,

What day it was I hardly can remember,
                  D   G
When down to the shipping office I went.
                                        D
That day there was a great demand for sailors,
                                  G
From the Colonies, from Frisco and from France,

So I shipped on board the liner named the Hotspur,
            D   G
And got paraletic drunk on my advance.

CHORUS:
          C   G
Oh Paddy lay back, take in your stack,
                                  D
Take a turn around the capstans heave up all,
G
About ships stations boys be handy,
                  D   G
For we're bound for Valporizor round the Horn.

Oh Paddy lay back (*Paddy lay back*) take in the stack (*take in the stack*)
Take a turn around the capstans heave up all (*heave up all*)
About ships stations boys be handy (*be handy*)
For we're bound for Valporizor round the Horn (*round the Horn*).

Now some of our fellows had been drinking (*been drinking*)
And me meself was heavy on the booze (*on the booze*)
So I sat upon me old sea chest a thinking (*a thinking*)
I'll just turn in and have meself a snooze (*have a snooze*).

Well I wished I was in the Jolly Sailors (*Sailors*)
Along with Irish Paddies drinking beer (*drinking beer*)
Then I thought what a jolly lot are sailors (*sailors*)
And with me flipper I wiped away a tear (*wiped a tear*).

THE GERMAN CLOCKWINDER

G
A German clockwinder

C
To Dublin once came,

D
Benjamin Fooks

C   G
Was the old German's name,

And as he was winding

C
His way round the strand,

D
He played on his flute

G
And the music was grand.

CHORUS:

G
Singing: Too-ra-lum-a-luma,

C
Too-ra-lum-a-luma-toor-a-de-ay,

D   G
Toor-a-de, toor-a-de, toor-a-de-ay,

Too-ra-lum-a-luma,

C
Too-ra-lum-a-luma-toor-a-de-ay,

D   G
Toor-a-de, Your-a-de-your-a-de-ay.

Oh there was a young lady
From Grosvenor Square,
Who said that her clock
Was in need of repair
In walks the bould German
And to her delight,
In less than five minutes
He had her clock right.
REPEAT CHORUS

Now as they were seated
Down on the floor
There came this very loud
Knock on the door
In walked her husband
And great was his shock
For to see the ould German
Wind up his wife's clock.
REPEAT CHORUS

The husband says he,
'Now look here Mary Anne
Don't let that bould German
Come in here again
He wound up your clock
And left mine on the shelf
If your oul' clock needs winding,
Sure I'll wind it meself.'
REPEAT CHORUS

GOD SAVE IRELAND

G
High upon the gallows tree

C   G
Swung the noble hearted three,

By the vengeful tyrant

D
Stricken in their bloom,

G
But they met him face to face

C   G
With the courage of the race,

And they went with souls

D   G
Undaunted to their doom.

CHORUS:

G
God save Ireland, said the heroes,

D
God save Ireland said they all,

G
Whether on the scaffold high

C   G
Or the battlefield we die,

Oh what matter

D   G
If for Ireland dear we fall.

Girt around with cruel foes,
Still their courage proudly rose,
For they thought of hearts
That loved them far and near;
Of the millions true and brave
O'er the ocean's swelling wave;
And the friend
Of holy Ireland ever dear.
REPEAT CHORUS

Climbed they up the rugged stair,
Rang their voices out in prayer,
Then with England's
Fatal cord around them cast,
Close beside the gallows tree,
Kissed like brothers lovingly,
True to home and faith
And freedom to the last.
REPEAT CHORUS

Never till the latest day
Shall the memory pass away,
O the gallant lives
Thus given for our land;
But on the cause must go
Amid joy or weal or woe,
Till we make our Isle
A nation free and grand.
REPEAT CHORUS